A HUNDRED DEVOTIONAL SONGS OF TAGORE

Rabindranath Tagore : Ardent Apostle of Devotion.
[*Courtesy* : Viswa Bharti, Ravindra Bhawan, Shantiniketan]

A Hundred Devotional Songs of Tagore

Mohit Chakrabarti

MOTILAL BANARSIDASS PUBLISHERS
PRIVATE LIMITED • DELHI

First Published: Delhi, 1999

ISBN: 81-208-1505-x (Cloth)
ISBN: 81-208-1687-0 (Paper)

Also available at:

MOTILAL BANARSIDASS

41 U.A. Bungalow Road, Jawahar Nagar, Delhi 110 007
8 Mahalaxmi Chamber, Warden Road, Mumbai 400 026
120 Royapettah High Road, Mylapore, Chennai 600 004
Sanas Plaza, 1302, Baji Rao Road, Pune 411 002
16 St. Mark's Road, Bangalore 560 001
8 Camac Street, Calcutta 700 017
Ashok Rajpath, Patna 800 004
Chowk, Varanasi 221 001

PRINTED IN INDIA
BY JAINENDRA PRAKASH JAIN AT SHRI JAINENDRA PRESS,
A-45 NARAINA, PHASE I, NEW DELHI 110 028
AND PUBLISHED BY NARENDRA PRAKASH JAIN FOR
MOTILAL BANARSIDASS PUBLISHERS PRIVATE LIMITED,
BUNGALOW ROAD, DELHI 110 007

Dedicated to

Sri Himadri Ranjan Bhattacharya
Professor of Education
Visva-Bharati University
Santiniketan

Sri Jagadindra Bhowmik
Eminent Tagore Scholar
Member, Board of Editors,
Rabindra-Rachanavali,
Government of West Bengal,
Calcutta

Dedicated to

Preface

To Rabindranath Tagore, devotion is like an *ektara* always playing on within. It is a state of mind—poignant and serene, joyous and simple—to be in unison with the All Beautiful.

A creator of no less than three thousand songs, Tagore is undeniably at his best when he composes devotional songs. In the quest for *maner manush,* his devotion finds a new language, a new rhythm, a new world of thought, feeling and emotion incomparable and beyond any parallel in depth and vision.

Here is a humble presentation of a hundred devotional songs of Tagore translated into English and preceded by the original ones in italics for the convenience of those who want to have a glimpse of the original. Moreover, the revered readers might tune on within themselves in moments of deep involvements with some of these devotional songs, and if so, perhaps therein lies the translator's success.

I cannot but recall the continual enthusiastic words of professor Himadri Ranjan Bhattacharya, my teacher and colleague, and the invaluable words of advice, tinged with love and affection, of Shri Jagadindra Bhowmik, a great Tagore scholar and member, Board of Editors, *Rabindra-Rachanavali.* I humbly dedicate this book to them as a token of my reverence and gratitude.

I would also like to convey my ardent gratefulness to Rabindra-Bhavana, Visva-Bharati, Santiniketan for the matter for illustration.

If the book appeals to everyone interested in devotional songs, I would feel my endeavour amply rewarded.

Mohit Chakrabarti

Seemantika
Seemanto Palli
Visva-Bharati University
Santiniketan-731 235 (INDIA)

Preface

Contents

A Note on Spirituality in the Devotional Songs of Rabindranath Tagore

Rabindranath Tagore is at his best in efflorescence of spirituality in his devotional songs. In these songs the spiritual concept of the All serene finds newer avenues in sorrows and sufferings, agonies and expectations, languishment and laughter. What brings forth a definite and distinct point of departure in the essence and ascent of spirituality is that he endearingly nursles optimism crystallized in the effulgence of purity and catholicity of vision. Even death becomes a caressing partner to encounter the All Beautiful. As he characteristically muses:

> If thy auspicious light is enkindled with
> the darkness of sorrow
> Let it be so.
> If death brings nearer the land of nectar
> Let it be so.

—*Duḥkher timire tumi,* p.1.
(Translated by me)

The spiritual vision of inner consciousness—to be in unison with the All serene—as Tagore reveals in his devotional songs, is the ardent prayer for a birth anew from the legion to the One. The prayer also finds a lucid language of welcome:

> Come ye to my heart in newer appearances
> Come with fragrance and colour, come with songs.
> Come with joyous touch in limbs
> Come with juicy laughter in the mind
> Come in closed eyes enamoured.
> Come with physique pure and bright,
> Come O beautiful refreshing and calm.
> Come O come in variegated dress.
> Come in joy and sorrow come in the core

Come daily in all activities
Come at the end of all work.

—*Tumi naba naba rūpe*, p. 10
(Translated by me)

Interestingly, Tagore does away with the intense and rigorous methods and techniques of spiritual poignance and loves to enjoy the warmth of spiritual freedom and spontaneity in day-to-day affairs of life. Love, to him, becomes an eternal gateway to the wonderland of spirituality. So is joy wherein he sincerely longs for unison with the All True amidst an aura of beauty all around:

With the light of the new sun awake today in joy anew in life pure and lovely, loving and shining and clean.
The new fountain of life is o'erflooded, the songs of hope surging.
In this air adorned with peace the fragrance of nectar-like flowers flows.

—*Naba ānande jāgo,* p. 24
(Translated by me)

How does Tagore come closer to the All Endearing? Here is an exquisite dramatic muse in which his sense of spirituality finds a living and thrilling resonance.

Yonder rings the sound of thy opening the door amidst my heart
If the bar is removed in thy room at night and at dawn
In what shame shall I then remain in my room.
Much have I said, lies are they all.
Much have I trekked, false are those trekkings.
At the end of all paths let me stand at thy door today—

—*Tomār duār kholār dhvani,* p. 42
(Translated by me)

To be christened with the spirituality of Tagore in the most intrinsic and poignant pattern is to muse and remuse his devotional songs, and, in doing so, one cannot but discover within oneself the lotus-land of spiritual excellence. Indeed, somewhere in the heartland of everyone lurks the unending beckoning of the All Beautiful in the soulful words of prayer:

This boon do I pray to thee, let me rise from death in the tunes of songs.

—*Tomār kāche e bar māgi*, p. 45
(Translated by me)

A few words about the basis and rationale of selection.

I have excluded the other writings of Tagore primarily because I would like to humbly present his genius and excellence in devotional songs—an illuminating area where, let us frankly admit, nothing is presented especially to the revered and interested readers of Tagore till now. The world of the songs of Tagore is too vast to be encompassed and appreciated either in translation or in critical appreciation, his entire writings notwithstanding. As such, selection is restricted to a hundred songs that reveal the diverse dimensions of devotion. This, however, does not at all eliminate the immense possibilities of unfolding the unparalleled genius of Tagore in his other devotional songs. Moreover, any selection including the present one always arrests every esteemed reader's attention on assessing the selector within a limited but definite and, therefore, existing parameter. If this axiom stands valid, I would really feel myself unerringly justified and amply rewarded.

Mohit Chakrabarti

Sources

No. 1. p. 1 Pūjā
No. 2. p. 2 "Kalpanā"
No. 3. p. 3 "Caṇdālikā"
No. 4. p. 4 Pūjā
No. 5. p. 5 Pūjā
No. 6. p. 6 Pūjā
No. 7. p. 7 Pūjā
No. 8. p. 8 Pūjā
No. 9. p. 9 Pūjā
No. 10. p. 10 "Gitāñjali
No. 11. p. 11 Pūjā
No. 12. p. 12 Pūjā
No. 13. p. 13 Pūjā
No. 14. p. 14 Pūjā
No. 15. p. 15 Pūjā
No. 16. p. 16 "Gītimālya"
No. 17. p. 17 "Gitāñjali-Gītimālya-Gītāli Saṁyojan"
No. 18. p. 18 Gītāñjali
No. 19. p. 19 "Gītāñjali-Gītimālya-Gītāli Saṁyojan"
No. 20. p. 20 "Gītāli"
No. 21. p. 21 Pūjā
No. 22. p. 22 "Gītimālya"
No. 23. p. 23 Pūjā
No. 24. p. 24 Pūjā
No. 25. p. 25 Pūjā
No. 26. p. 26 "Gītāñjali"
No. 27. p. 27 "Gītāñjali"
No. 28. p. 28 "Gītāñjali"
No. 29. p. 29 "Gītāli"
No. 30. p. 30 "Gītāli"
No. 31. p. 31 "Gītimālya"
No. 32. p. 32 Pūjā
No. 33. p. 33 "Gītāli"

No. 34. p. 34 "Gītāli"
No. 35. p. 35 "Gītāli"
No. 36. p. 36 "Gītāñjali-Gītīmālya-Gītāli Saṁyojan"
No. 37. p. 37 "Gītāli"
No. 38. p. 38 "Gītāli"
No. 39. p. 39 "Gītāli"
No. 40. p. 40 "Gītāli"
No. 41. p. 41 "Gītāli"
No. 42. p. 42 "Gītāli"
No. 43. p. 43 "Gītāli"
No. 44. p. 44 "Gītāli"
No. 45. p. 45 "Gītāli"
No. 46. p. 46 "Gītāli"
No. 47. p. 47 "Gītāli"
No. 48. p. 48 "Gītāli"
No. 49. p. 49 "Gītāli"
No. 50. p. 50 "Gītāli"
No. 51. p. 51 "Gītāli"
No. 52. p. 52 "Gītāli"
No. 53. p. 53 "Gītāli"
No. 54. p. 54 "Phālgunī"
No. 55. p. 55 "Phālgunī"
No. 56. p. 56 "Phālgunī"
No. 57. p. 57 "Pūjā"
No. 58. p. 58 "Pūjā"
No. 59. p. 59 "Pūjā"
No. 60. p. 60 "Pūjā"
No. 61. p. 61 "Pūjā"
No. 62. p. 62 "Pūjā"
No. 63. p. 63 "Pūjā"
No. 64. p. 64 "Pūjā"
No. 65. p. 65 "Pūjā"
No. 66. p. 66 "Pūjā"
No. 67. p. 67 "Pūjā"
No. 68. p. 68 "Pūjā"
No. 69. p. 69 "Arūpratan"
No. 70. p. 70 "Arūpratan"
No. 71. p. 71 "Arūpratan"
No. 72. p. 72 "Pūjā"

No. 73. p. 73 "Arūpratan"
No. 74. p. 74 "Pūjā"
No. 75. p. 75 "Muktadhārā"
No. 76. p. 76 "Muktadhārā"
No. 77. p. 77 "Caṇḍālikā"
No. 78. p. 78 Pūjā
No. 79. p. 79 "Gītāli"
No. 80. p. 80 "Gītāli"
No. 81. p. 81 "Gītāli"
No. 82. p. 82 "Gītāli"
No. 83. p. 83 "Gītāli"
No. 84. p. 84 "Gītāli"
No. 85. p. 85 "Gītāli"
No. 86. p. 86 "Gītāli"
No. 87. p. 87 "Gītāli"
No. 88. p. 88 "Gītimālya"
No. 89. p. 89 "Gītimālya"
No. 90. p. 90 "Gītimālya"
No. 91. p. 91 "Gītimālya"
No. 92. p. 92 "Gītimālya"
No. 93. p. 93 "Gītimālya"
No. 94. p. 94 "Gītimālya"
No. 95. p. 95 "Gītimālya"
No. 96. p. 96 "Gītimālya"
No. 97. p. 97 "Gītimālya"
No. 98. p. 98 "Gītimālya"
No. 99. p. 99 "Gītimālya"
No. 100. p. 100 "Gītimālya"

1

If thy auspicious light

Duḥkher timire yadi jvale taba maṅgal-ālok
Tabe tāi hok.
Mṛtyu yadi kāche āne tomār amṛtamay lok
Tabe tāi hok.
Pūjār pradīpe taba jvale yadi mama dīpta śok
Tabe tāi hok.
Aśru-āṁkhī-pare yadi phuṭe othe taba sneha cokh
Tabe tāi hok.

If thy auspicious light is enkindled with the darkness of sorrow
Let it be so.
If death brings nearer thy land of nectar
Let it be so.
If my enlightened bereavement is brimmed on with thy lamp of worship
Let it be so.
If thy affectionate eyes bloom on the tearful eyes
Let it be so.

2

From fear unto thy fearlessness

Bhay hate taba abhayamajhe nūtana janama dāo he.
Dīnatā hate akṣay dhane, saṁśay-hate satyasadane.
Jaḍatā hate nabīna jībane nūtana janama dāo he.
Āmāra icchā haite prabhu, tomāra icchāmājhe–
Āmāra svārtha haite prabhu, taba maṅgalakāje–
Aneka haite eker ḍore, sukha dukha hate śāntikroḍe–
Āmā hate nātha, tomāte more nūtana janama dāo he.

From fear into thy fearlessness, O give me new life
From poverty to eternal wealth, from doubt to the temple of Truth
From passivity to life anew O give me new life
From my desire O Lord, to thy desire
From my cause O Lord, to thy auspicious service
From the legion to the unison of One, from pleasure and pain to the lap of peace—
From me, O Lord, to thee, give me new life.

3

Blessed am I, says the flower

Phul bale, dhanya āmi māṭir pare,
Debatā ogo tomār sebā āmār ghare.
Janma niyechi dhūlite dayā kare dāo bhulite
Nāi dhūli mor antare.
Nayan tomār nata karo.
Dalguli kāṁpe tharotharo.
Caraṇaparaś diyo diyo, dhūlir dhanke karo svargiya—
Dharār praṇām āmi tomār tare.

Blessed am I, says the flower, on the earth.
O God, thy service is in my room.
On the dust am I born kindly allow me to forget,
No dust is there in my heart.
Bend thy eyes,
The petals tremble.
Give, give the touch of thy feet
Make the wealth of dust divine—
I, the salute of the earth, am at thy service.

4

Tell me not to work today

Ājke more bolonā kāj karte
Yabā āmi dekhāśonār nepathye āj sarte
Ksaṇik maraṇ marte
Acin kūle pāḍi deba, ālokloke janma neba,
Maraṇrase alakhjhorāy prāṇer kalas bharte.
Anek kāler kannahāsir chāyā
Dharuk sāṁjher raṅgin megher māyā.
Ājke nāhay ekṭi belā chāḍba māṭir deher khelā,
Gāner deśe yābo uḍe surer deha dharte.

Tell me not to work today.
Behind the curtain of care shall I go.
To die for a momentary death.
To the unknown shore shall I cross, to the land of Light shall I be born
To fill in the pitcher of life with the nectar of death in the fountain unseen
Let the shadow of laughter and tears long ago
Be enamoured with the colourful clouds of the evening.
For a few hours today shall I, however, leave the physical game on this earth
Away shall I fly to the land of the muse to catch hold of the body of the tune.

5

What a beauty have ye shown

Āji Śubha Śubhra prāte kibā śobhā dekhāle
Śantirlok jyotirlok prakāśi.
Nikhil nīl ambar bidāriyā dikdigante
Ābariyā rabi śaśī tārā
Puṇyamahimā uṭhe bibhāsi.

What a beauty have ye shown today in the
auspicious white morning
By manifesting the world of peace,
the world of lustre !
Piercing the universal blue firmament
Covering the horizon with all directions
by the sun, the moon and the stars
Thy auspicious glory shines out in efflorescence.

6

With thy name have I opened my eyes

Tomāri nāme nayan melinu puṇyaprabhāte āji,
Tomāri nāme khulila hṛdayśatadal dalarāji.
Tomāri nāme nibiḍ timire phuṭila kanaklekhā,
Tomāri nāme uṭhila gagane kiraṇbīṇā bāji.
Tomāri nāme pūrbatoraṇe khulia siṁhadvār,
Bāhirila rabi nabīn āloke dīpta mukut māji.
Tomāri nāme jībansāgare jāgila laharīlīlā,
Tomāri nāme nikhil bhuban bāhire āsila sāji.

With thy name have I opened my eyes on the auspicious morning today,
With thy name the petals of the lotus of my heart are bloomed.
With thy name are deciphered the golden writings in deep darkness,
With thy name the *veena* of lustre plays on.
With thy name the golden gate is opened in the eastern fortress.
In lustre anew the sun came out by cleaning the shining headdress.
With thy name the play of waves surged on in the sea of life.
With thy name did the universe come out in adornment.

7

O Lord of my heart

Man prān kaḍiyā lao he hṛdaysvāmī,
Saṁsārer sukh dukh sakali bhuliba āmi.
Sakal sukh dāo tomār premasukhe—
Tumi jāgi thāko jībane dinayāmī.

O Lord of my heart, snatch away my mind and life
All pleasures and pains of the would I forget.
With thy pleasures of happiness give me all the happiness
In my life do thou remain awake, O awakener of the day.

8

All my truth and falsehood

Āmār satya mithyā sakali bhulāye dāo
Āmāy ānande bhāsāo
Nā cāhi tarka nā cāhi yukti, nā jāni bandha nā jāni mukti.
Tomār biśvabyāpinī icchā āmār antare jāgāo
Sakal biśva dubiyā yāk śāntipāthāre,
sab sukh dukh thamiyā yāk hṛdaymājhāre
Sakal bākya sakal śabda sakal ceṣṭa hauk stabdha—
Tomār cittajayinī bāṇī āmār antare śunāo

All my truth and falsehood do thou make me forget,
In joy do thou make me float,
Arguments I want not, nor do I want reasonings,
Yoke I know not, not do I know freedom,
Awake in my heart thy world embracing desire,
Let the whole universe be immersed in the sea of peace,
Let all the happiness and sufferings come to a stop amid the heart.
Let all thy sentences and words, all endeavour become silent—
Make me listen to my heart thy heart-winning message.

9

With the touch of thy feet

Hṛday-ābaraṇ khule gela tomār padaparaśe harașe ohe
doyāmay
Antare bāhire herinu tomāre
Loke loke, dike dike, āṁdhāre āloke, sukhe dukhe—
Herinu he ghare pare, jagatmoy cittamay.

With the touch of thy feet, O Lord of kindness,
With thy laughter the veil of my heart is opened
Behold I in and out my heart thee
From man to man, towards every direction,
in light and darkness
in sorrow and happiness
Do I behold thee in the room, throughout the world, all
through the mind.

10

Come ye to my heart

Tumi naba naba rūpe eso prāṇe,
Eso gandhe baraṇe eso gāne.
Eso aṅge pulakmay paraśe,
Eso citte sudhāmay haraṣe,
Eso mugdha mudita dunayāne.
Eso nirmala ujjvala kānta,
Eso sundara snigdha praśanta.
Eso eso he bicitra bidhāne.
Eso duḥkhe sukhe, eso marme,
Eso nitya nitya sab karme,
Eso sakal karma-abasāne.

Come ye to my heart in newer appearance
come with fragrance and colour, come with songs.
come with joyous touch in limbs
come with juicy laughter in the mind
come in closed eyes enamoured.
Come with physique pure and bright,
Come O beautiful refreshing and calm,
Come O come in variegated dress.
come in joy and sorrow come in the core
come daily in all activities,
come at the end of all work.

11

With silent drops

Śānti karo bariṣan nīrab dhāre nāth, cittamājhe
Sukhe dukhe sab kāje, nirjane janasamāje.
Udita rākho nāth, tomār premacandra
Animeṣ mama locane gabhīratimiramājhe.

With silent drops, O Lord, shower peace amid the mind
In joy and sorrow in every work, alone in the human society.
Keep thy loving moon arisen
In my eyes staring amidst poignant darkness.

12

Who called O Lord

Duḥkharāte he nāth, ke dākile—
Jāgi herinu taba premamukhachabi
Herinu ūṣāloke biśva taba kole,
Jāge taba nayane prāte śubhra rabi.
Śuninu bạne upabane ānandagāthā,
Āśā hṛdaye bahi nitya gāne kabi.

Who called O Lord, on the night of sorrow—
Being awakened, the picture of thy loving countenance did I behold
In the light of dawn did I behold the universe on thy lap,
The clear sun awakes in thy eyes in the morning
The choric song of joy did I listen in the forest and in the wood
With hopes treasured in the heart the poet sings unendingly.

13

O who came to my temple

Mandire mama ke āsila he!
Sakal gagan amṛtamagan,
Diśi diśi gela miśi amāniśi dūre dūre
Sakal duār āpani khulila,
Sakal pradīp āpani jvalila,
Sab bīṇā bājila naba naba sure sure.

O who come to my temple !
Immersed in nectar is all the sky
To the distant did the dark night come in unison towards diverse directions.
Every door automatically opened
Every lamp trimmed by itself
All the *veenas* played on with newer tunes.

14

Empty handed, O Lord

Śūnya hāte phiri he nāth, pathe pathe—phiri he dvāre dvāre
Cirabhikhārī hṛdi mama niśidin cāhe kāre
Citta nā śānti jāne, tṛṣñā nā tṛpti māne—
Yāhā pāi tāi hārāi, bhāsi aśrudhāre
Sakal yātrī cali gela bahi gela sab belā
Āse timirayāminī, bhāngiyā gelo melā—
Kata path āche bāki, yābo cale bhikṣā rākhī,
Kothā jvale gṛhapradīp kon sindhupāre

Empty handed, O Lord, do I tread on every path—tread from door to door
Whom does my mind desire day and night—a beggar eternal
Mind knows not peace, contentment does thirst accept—
I lose whatever I receive, in the stream of tears do I float.
All the travellers departed, the day did wane away
The dark night did step in, the congregation broke apart—
How endless remains the path, leaving the alms, shall I depart,
On the shores of the sea unknown the lamp of the room is in effulgence beyond my knowledge.

15

With what pretext

Āmāre tumī kiser chaḷe pāṭhāle dūre,
Ābār āmi caraṇatale āsiba ghure.
Sohāg kare karicba helā ṭāniba ba'le ditecha ṭhelā
He rājā, taba keman khelā rājya juḍe

With what pretext will ye send me away
At thy feet shall I come back again.
In affection art thou ignoring me, and pushing me only to pull
O King, what game is going on all through thy kingdom.

16

Where on the sea-shore

Rātri ese yethāy meśe diner pārābāre
Tomāy āmāy dekhā hala sei mohānār dhāre.
Seikhānete sāday kāloy mile geche āṁdhār āloy—
Seikhānete dheu chuṭeche a pāre oi pāre
Nitalnīl nīrab-mājhe bājlo gabhīr bāṇī,
Nikaṣete uṭhla phuṭe sonār rekhākhāni.
Mukher pāne tākāte yāi, dekhi dekhi dekhte nā pāi—
Svapan-sāthe jaḍiye jāgā, kṁādi ākul dhāre.

Where on the sea-shore of the day the night does unite,
On that very space do we two meet
Amid darkness and light there is the unison of the white and the black
Waves have rolled on there towards the shores.
In the deep blue silence the poignant message did spring forth
The golden line was in efflorescence out of darkness
Towards the countenance do I want to look, I am about to see but I can't see—
It's awakening in the midst of dream, with streams of tears do I weep.

17

O my Lord, my dear

Prabhu āmār, priya āmār param dhan he
Cirapather saṅgī āmār cirajīban he.
Tṛpti āmār, atṛpti mor, mukti āmār, bandhanaḍor,
Duḥkhasukher caram āmār jīban maraṇ he.
Āmār sakal gatir mājhe param gati he,
Nitya premer dhāme āmār param gati he,
Ogo sabār, ogo āmār, biśva hate citte bihār
Antabihīn līlā tomār nūtan nūtan he

O my Lord, my dear, my great wealth
My companion to the path unending, my life eternal.
My contentment as well as dissipation, freedom of mine as well as strings of enchantment
The climax of my sorrow and happiness, O my life and death
O the most adored of all my destinations
O the most endeared lover in the abode of eternal love
O ye mine and of all, travel in the mind from the universe—
Thy *lila* is unending, O new, ever new.

18

With one salute, O Lord

Ekṭi namaskāre prabhu, ekṭi namaskāre
Sakal deha luṭiye paḍuk tomār e saṁsāre.
Ghana śrābaṇmegher mata raser bhāre namro nata
Ekṭi namaskāre prabhu, ekṭi namaskāre
Samasta man paḍiyā thāk taba bhabandāre
Nānā surer ākul dhārā miliye diye ātmahārā
Ekti namaskāre prabhu, ekṭi namaskāre
Samasta gān samāpta hok nīrab pārābāre
Haṁsa yeman mānasyātrī temni sārā dibasrātri
Ekṭi namaskāre prabhu, ekṭi namaskāre
Samasta prāṇ uḍe caluk mahāmaran-pāre

With one salute, Lord, with one salute
Let the whole body prostrate in this world of thine
Benign and bent down with the burden of juice like the dense cloud of *sravan*
With one salute Lord, with one salute
Let the whole mind remain awaiting at the door of thy residence
Being lost within the self through unison of flooded streams of diverse tunes
With one salute, Lord, with one salute
Let all songs end in the silent sea
All day and night like a swan travelling in the mind
With one salute, Lord, with one salute
Let the whole heart travel aflying over the sea of great death.

19

Awake in eyes distinct

Jāgo nirmal netre rātrir parapāre,
Jāgo antaraketre muktir adhikāre.
Jāgo bhaktir tīrthe pūjāpusper ghrāṇe,
Jāgo unmukhacitte, jāgo amlānaprāṇe,
Jāgo nandananṛtye sudhāsindhur dhāre,
Jāgo svārther prānte premamandiradvāre.
Jāgo ujjval puṇye, jāgo nīścal āśe.
Jāgo niḥsim śūnye pūrṇer bāhupāśe
Jāgo nirbhayadhāme, Jāgo saṁgrāmasāje,
Jāgo brahmer nāmejāgo kalyāṇakāje
Jāgo durgamayātrī duḥkher abhisāre,
Jāgo svārther prāntepremamandiradvāre.

Awake in eyes distinct on the other shore of night
Awake in the arena of the mind in the depth of freedom.
Awake in the pilgrimage of devotion in the fragrance of
the flowers of worship.
Awake with mind aquivered, awake with a heart serene
Awake in dance aesthetic beside the sea of juice,
Awake on the edge of the self at the door of the temple
of love
Awake with virtue resplendant, awake with hope unmoved
Awake in the endless void in the embraces of fulness
Awake in the abode of fearlessness, awake in the robe of
struggle
Awake in the name of the Brahma, awake in auspicious
deeds.
Awake O traveller unknown in the adventure of sorrow,
Awake on the edge of the self at the door of the temple
of love.

20

If sorrow does embrace you not

Duḥkha yadi nā pābe to duḥkha tomār ghuche kabe.
Biṣke biṣer dāha diye dahan kare mārte habe
Jvalte de tor āguṇṭāre bhay kichu nā karis tāre,
Chāi haye se nibhbe yakhan jvalbe nā ār kabhu tabe.
Eḍiye tāṁre pālās nā re; dharā dite hos nā kātar.
Dīrgha pathe chuṭe kebal dīrgha karis duḥkhaṭā tor.
Marte marte maraṇṭāre śeṣ kare de ekebāre,
Tār pare sei jīban ese āpan āsan āpni labe.

If sorrow does embrace you not, when would your sorrow depart?
Poison would have to be killed with the fire of poison.
Let the fire in you be allowed to be lit,
be not afraid of it.
No more would it burn once it is put off in ashes.
Run not away evading Him, feel not uneasy to submit
Lengthen alone your sorrow by trekking on the long path
Bring death totally to an end by death unending
Life then would come and automatically take his seat.

21

Day and night look

Niśidin cāhore tṁār pāne
Bikaśibe prāṇ tṁār guṇagāne
Hero re antare se mukh sundar
Bholo duḥkha tṁār premamadhupāno.

Day and night look at His countenance
With His auspicious song life will be in efflorescence
Look in your heart that lovely countenance
Forget sorrow by drinking the juice of His love.

22

I've got my leave

Peyechi chuṭi, bidāy debo bhāi—
Sabāre āmi praṇām kare yāi.
Phirāye dinu dvārer cābi, rākhi nā ār gharer dābi—
Sabār āji prasādbāṇī cāi.
Anek din chilām pratibeśī,
Diyechi yata niyechi tār beśi.
Prabhāt haye eseche rāti, nibiyā gela koṇer bāti—
Paḍeche dāk, calechi āmi tāi.

I've got my leave, bid me farewell O brother
I depart with salutes to all.
I've given back the keys of the room, no more claim do I have for it —
The message of contentment from everyone do I pray for.
Long did I enjoy neighbourhood
I've received more than what I've offered.
The night is about to beckon the morning, the lamp in the corner is extinguished
The call is there and so am I bidding good-bye.

23

The sea of peace thou art

Śāntisamudra tumi gabhīr,
Ati agādh ānandarāśi
Tomāte sab duḥkhajvālā
Kari nirbāṇ bhuliba saṁsār,
Asīm sukhasāgare dube yāba.

The sea of peace thou art fathomless,
Ample joy very unending
All sorrows and sufferings shall I entrust upon thee
With emancipation shall I forget the world
In the endless sea of happiness shall I immerse.

24

With the light of the new sun

Naba ānande jāgo āji nabarabikiraṇe
Śubhra sundar prīti ujjval nirmal jībane.
Utsārita naba jībananirjhar ucchvāsita āśāgīti,
Amṛtapuṣpagandha babe āji ei śāntipabane.

With the tight of the new sun awake today in joy anew
In life pure and lovely, loving and shining and clean
The new fountain of life is o'erflooded, the songs of hope surging
In this air adorned with peace the fragrance of nectar like flowers flows.

25

Let me receive thy kindness

Hṛdaye tomār dayā jena pāi
Saṁsāre yā dibe māniba tāi,
Hṛdaye dayā yena pāi
Taba dayā jāgibe smaraṇe
Niśidin jībane maraṇe
Duhke sukhe sampade bipade tomāri dayā-pāne cāi —
Tomāri dayā yena pāi
Taba dayā śānti nīre antare nāmibe dhīre.
Taba dayā maṅgala-ālo
Jīban āṁdhāre jvālo —
Premabhakti mama sakal śakti mama tomāri dayārūpe pāi
Āmār bale kichu nāi.

Let me receive thy kindness in my heart
Whate'er will ye offer me in the world shall I accept
Let me receive kindness in my heart.
In remembrance will thy kindness awake
All day and night in life and death
In joy and sorrow, wealth and adversitv do I behold at thy kindness —
Let me receive thy kindness.
Slowly will thy kindness stream down in the water of peace
Let thy kindness trim on the aura of goodness
in the darkness of life.
My love and devotion all my power do I receive in the form of thy kindness alone
Nothing do I have as my own.

26

It won't be

Amaṇ ādāl diye lukiye gele calbe nā.
Ebār hṛday-mājhe lukiye boso, keu jānbe nā, keu balbe nā.
biśve tomār lukocuri deś-bideśe katai ghuri —
Ebār bolo āmār maner koṇe debe dharā, calbe nā.
Jāni āmār kaṭhin hṛdaẏ caraṇ rakhār yogya se nay —
Sakhā, tomār hāoyā lāgle hiyāy tabu ki prāṇ galbe nā.
nāhay āmār nāi sādhanā - jharle tomār kṛpār kaṇā
Takhan nimeṣe ki phutbe nā phul, cakite phal phalbe nā?

It won't do if thou dost pass on hiding in such a back-drop
Have thy seat now a-hiding amidst the heart, none would know, none would say.
Thy hide and seek is all thro' the world, what a round do I make at home and abroad —
Tell me now that thou wouldst be there in the corner of my heart and wouldst not play trickeries with me.
Know I that my hard heart is not worthy of placing thy feet.
Friend, wouldn't the heart melt with the touch of thy wind. May be that no pursuit do I have. If the shower of thy pity does descend
Wouldn't the flower bloom all of a sudden, the fruit be brought forth within a flash ?

27

If, my Lord

Yadi tomār dekhā nā pāi prabhu, ebār e jībane
Tabe tomāy āmi pāi ni yena se kathā ray mane.
Yena bhule nā yāi, bedanā pāi śayane svapane.
E saṁsārer hāṭe
Āmār yatai dibas kāṭe,
Āmār yatai duhāt bhare uṭhe dhane
Tabu kichui āmi pāi ni yena se kathā ray mane.
Yena bhule nā yāi, bedanā pāi śayane svapane.
Yadi ālasbhare
Āmi basi pather pare,
Yadi dhūlāy śayan pāti sajatane
Yena sakal pathi bāki āche se kathā ray mane.
Yena bhule nā yāi, bedanā pāī śayane svapane
Yatai uṭhe hāsi
Ghare Yatai bāje bṁāśi Ogo yatai gṛha sājāi āyojane,
Yena tomāy ghare hay ni ānā se kathā ray mane.
Yena bhule nā yāi, bedanā pāi śayane svapane.

If, my Lord, do I now fail to encounter thee in this life
I did not have ye then, let this be noted in the mind.
Let me not forget that, let me be prized with pain in sleep and dream.
In the fare of this world
The more do my days wane
The more my two hands are heaped with wealth
Yet did I have nothing, let this be noted in the mind.
Let me not forget that.....

If in idleness
Do I sit on the path
If do I spread the bed with care on the dust
All paths are as it were yet to be trodden, let this be noted in the mind.
Let me not forget that.....
The more laughter surges on
The more the flute in the room plays on
The more, O dear, do I decorate the room in arrangements
I have failed to bring thee in my room, let this be noted in the mind.
Let me not forget that.....

28

Lord, eyes awake for thee

Prabhu, tomā lāgi āṁkhi jāge;
Dekhā nāi pāi
Path cāi,
seo mane bhālo lāge.
Dhūlāte bosiyā dāre bhikhārī hṛdoy hā re
Tomāri karuṇa māge; Kṛpā nāi pāi
Śudhu cāi,
Seo mane bhālo lāge
Āji e jagatmājhe kata sukhe kata kāje
Cale gela sabe āge; Sāthī nāi pāi
Tomāy cāi
Seo mane bhālo lāge
Cāri dike sudhā-bharā byākul śyāmal dharā
Kṁādāy re anurāge;
Byātha pāi,
Seo mane bhālo lāge.

Lord, eyes awake for thee
I've failed to encounter thee, I await the meeting
That, too, is pleasing to my mind.
Sitting on the dust at the doorsteps the beggar-like mind, alas,
Prays for thy pity, Blessings do I have not have I simply pray,
That , too, is pleasing to my mind.
Amid this world today with happiness unlimited and work unending.

All have departed first. No companion do I have. Thee
do I want
That too is pleasing to my mind
All around the restless green earth filled in with the
juice
In devotion, ah, does make one weep
I've failed to encounter thee
I ache
That, too, is pleasing to my mind.

29

Why will ye keep me

Sukhe āmāy rākhbe kena, rākho tomār kole.
Yāk-nā go sukh jvale.
Yāk-nā pāyer talār māṭi. tumi takhan dharbe āṁṭi—
Tule niye dulābe oi bāhudolār dole.
Yekhāne ghar bṁādhba āmi āse āsuk bān—
Tumi yadi bhāsāo more cāi ne paritrāṇ.
Hār menechi miṭeche bhay-tomār jay to āmāri jay
Dharā deba, tomāy āmi dharba ye tāi hale.

Why will ye keep me in happiness, on thy lap do ye keep
O let all happiness be burnt away.
Let the earth for footings be slipped away, thou wilt clasp me then.
On the swings of thy arms do thou swing me on.
Let the tide come, if it comes, where my nest shall I build
No survival do I desire if thou maketh me float.
Defeat have I accepted, fear have I come over—thy victory is indeed the victory of mine
I shall surrender for that would allow me to hold on thee.

30

Let all the enlivening dream

Āmār sakal raser dhārā
Tomāte āj hok-nā hārā
Jīban juḍe lāguk paraś, bhuban byepe jāguk haraṣ,
Tomār rūpe maruk dube āmār duṭi āṁkhitārā.
Hāriye-yāoya manṭi āmār
Phiriye tumi ānle ābār
Chadiye-paḍā āśāguli kuḍiye tumi lao go tuli,
Galār hāre dolāo tāre gṁāthā tomār kare sārā

Let all the enlivening dream in me
Be lost in thee.
Let the touch be all thro' the life, let laughter endear all
thro' the earth
Let the stars of my two eyes be drowned in thy beauty.
Thou hast brought back
My mind that is lost
O thou wouldst pick up the hopes scattered,
Swing these in the necklace after thy sewing is over.

31

Thou hast remained standing

Dm̐āḍiye ācho tumi āmār gāner o pāre—
Āmār surguli pāy caraṇ, āmi pāi ne tomāre.
Bātās bahe mari mari, ār bm̐edhe rekho nā tarī—
Eso eso pār haye mor hṛdaymājhāre.
Tomār sāthe gāner khelā dūrer khelā ye,
Bedanāte bm̐āśi bājāy sakal belā ye.
Kabe niye āmār bm̐āśi bājābe go āpni āsi
Ānandamay nīrab rāter nibiḍ ām̐dhāre.

Thou hast remained standing on the other bank of my song
My tunes beget feet, I fail to have thee
O what a wind blows, fasten not the boat any more—
Come O come sailing along in the midst of my heart.
With thee is my play of songs and distance
All day long the flute plays on in pain
When wouldst thou come of thy own with my flute playing on
In the poignant darkness of night joyous and silent.

32

No fear, no fear in this world

Saṁsāre kono bhay nāhi nāhi—
Ore bhaycañcala prāṇ , jībane maraṇe sabe
Rayechi tṁāhāri dvāre.
Abhayaśaṅkha bāje nikhil ambare sugambhīr.
Diśi diśi dibāniśi sukhe śoke
Lok-lokāntare.

No fear, no fear in this world
O life restless in fear, all in life and death.
At His door alone have we remained
The fearless conch-shell plays on in poignance
In the world and in the sky
In every direction day and night in happiness and sorrow
In human habitation and beyond.

33

No end is there

Śeṣ nāhi ye, Śeṣ kathā ke balbe
Āghāt haye dekha dila, āgun haye jvalbe.
Sāṅga hale megher pālā suru habe bṛsti ḍhālā
Baraph jamā sārā hale nadī haye galbe.
Phurāy yā tā phurāy sudhu cokhe
Andhakārer periye duār yāy cole āloke
Purātaner hṛday ṭuṭe āpni nūtan uṭhbe phuṭe
Jībane phul phoṭā hale maraṇe phal phalbe.

No end is there, who will tell the last word
Like a stroke did it appear, like fire will it trim.
With the end of the trailing of cloud the pouring of rainfall would start
With the end of freezing of ice will it melt down in the form of a river
What ends in eyes alone does it end
Crossing the doors of darkness does it depart in light
Tearing off the heart of the old does the new bloom forth itself
At the end of the blooming of flowers in life, the fruit will appear in death.

34

No, O no

Nā re, nā re, habe nā tor svargasādhan—
Sekhāne ye madhur beśe phm̐ād peta ray sukher bm̐ādhan
Bhebechili diner śeṣe tapta pather prānte ese
Sonār meghe miliye yābe sārā diner sakal km̐ādan.
Nā re, nā re, habe nā tor, habe nā tā—
Sandhyātārār hāsir nīce habe nā tor śayan pātā.
Pathik bm̐adhu pāgal kare pathe bāhir karbe tore—
Hṛday ye tor pheṭe giye phuṭbe tabe tm̐ār ārādhan.

No, O no, thy pursuit of heaven will not happen.
The string of happiness spreads trap in a pleasant appearance
Thought ye that at the day's end on the edge of the heated path
All the day-long cries will in the golden cloud be in unison.
No, O no, that won't be for ye, that won't be—
Beneath the laughter of the evening star, thy bed will not be spread o'er
The traveller bride would make thee mad and out in the streets would make thee.
Bursting open thy heart, His devotion would blossom forth.

35

Flooding this sweetness

Tomār ei mādhurī chāpiye ākāś jharbe,
Āmār prāṇe naile se ki kothāo dharbe.
Ei-ye ālo sūrye grahe tārāy jhare paḍe śatalakṣha dhārāy
Pūrṇa habe e prāṇ yakhan bharbe
Tomār phule ye raṅ ghumer mato lāgla.
Āmār mane lege tabe se ye jāgla
Ye prem kṁāpāy bisvabiṇāy pulake saṁgīte se uṭhbe bhese palake
Ye din āmār sakal hṛday harbe.

Flooding this sweetness thine the sky will pour forth,
Would it otherwise in my heart contain anywhere?
This light in the sun, in the planet and in the stars
Beaming forth in hundreds and millions of streams
Would end in fullness with the fullness of this life
Like a slumber the colour that touched thy flowers
Touching my mind did it spring forth
The love that in thrill does vibrate the global *veena* would in a moment be flash afloating in songs.
On the day when all my heart will it steal away.

36

Eternal is not thy sorrow

Duḥkha ye tor nay re cirantan—
Pār āche re ei sāgarer bipul krandan
Ei jībaner byathā yata eikhāne sab habe gata,
Ciraprāṇer ālay-mājhe bipul sāntan.
Maraṇ ye tor nay re cirantan—
Duār tāhār periye yābi, chṁiḍbe re bandhan.
E belā tor yadi jhaḍe pūjār kusum jhare paḍe,
Yābār belāy bharbe thālāy mālā o candan.

Eternal is not thy sorrow
The vast cry of this sea has its shores.
All the pains of this life will all diminish here
Amid the abode of eternal life is unending consolation.
Eternal is not thy death—
Thou wouldst cross her door, all strings would be torn apart
If now thy flowers of worship wither away in storm,
Garlands and sandalwood paste would fill in the tray at the time of parting.

37

Hold on this

Ei kathāṭā dhare rākhis-mukti tore petei habe.
Ye path geche pārer pāne se pathe tor jetei habe.
Abhay mane kanṭha chādi gān geye tui dibi pādi,
Khuśi haye jhaḍer hāoyāy ḍheu ye tore khetei habe.
Pāker ghore ghoray yadi, chuṭi tore petei habe.
Calār pathe kṁātā thāke, dale tomāy yetei habe.
Sukher āśā āṁkḍe laye maris ne tui bhaye bhaye,
Jībanke tor bhare nite maraṇ-āghāt khetei habe.

Hold on this that emancipation is a must for you.
The path towards the shore is a must for you.
In a fearless mind and with a full-throated voice you'd cross over singing
In a pleasing mind amid amid the stormy wind, wave to embrace is a must for you.
In the whirlpool of silt, deliverance is a must for you.
Trampling the thorns on the way is a must for you.
Clasping the hopes of happiness die not in utter fear,
To fill in life, the stroke of death is a must for you.

38

Be easy, be easy

Sahaj habi, sahaj habi, ore man, sahaj habi—
Kācher jinis dūre rākhe tār theke tui dūre rabi
Keno re tor du hāt pātā — dān to nā cāi, cāi ye dātā—
Sahaje tui dibi yakhan sahaje tui sakal labi
Sahaj habi, sahaj habi, ore man, sahaj habi —
Āpan bacan-racan hate bāhir haye āy re kabi
Sakal kathār bāhirete bhuban āche hṛday pete,
Nīrab phuler nayan-pāne ceye āche prabhāt-rabi.

Be easy, be easy, O mind, easy be—
Things nearby keep one apart, keep yourself off from their company
Why are your two hands unfolded-gifts do I not want, donor do I honour
When you will at ease take, you will then offer easily
Be easy, be easy, O mind, easy be—
From composing words of your own, O Poet, make thee free
Apart from words in legion the world does the heart adorn
The morning sun looks at the eyes of the silent flowers staringly.

39

O coward

Ore bhīru, tomār hāte nāi bhubaner bhār.
Hāler kāche mājhi āche, karbe tarī pār,
Tuphān yadi ese thāke tomār kiser dāy —
Ceye dekho ḍheuyer khelā, kaj ki bhābanāy.
Āsuk-nāko gahan rāti, hok-nā andhakār —
Hāler kāche mājhi āche, karbe tarī pār.
Paścime tui tākiye dekhis meghe ākāś dobā,
Ānande tui puber dike dekh-nā tārār śobhā.
Sāthī yārā āche tārā tomār āpan bale
Bhāba ki tāi rakṣā pābe tomāri oi kole.
Uṭhbe re jhaḍ, dulbe re buk, jāgbe hāhākār—
Haler kāche mājhi āche, karbe tarī pār.

O coward, the burden of the world rests not on you
The oarsman is nearby the oars, and he'll sail the boat
across.
If the gale comes what worry do you have
Behold the play of waves, what's the use of thoughts?
Let the dense night come, let darkness be dominant—
The oarsman is nearby the ours, and he'll sail the boat
across.
Behold the western sky immersed in the cloud
Just behold in joy the beauty of stars in the east
As the comrades you have are your own
Do you think that they are assured of safely in your lap?
The storms will start, the heart will swing, agonies will
wail
The oarsman is nearby the oars, and he'll sail the boat
across.

40

How do you play on

Agnibīṇā bājāo tumi keman kare,
Ākāś kṁāpe tārār ālor gāner ghore.
Temni kare āpan hāte chṁule āmār bedonāte,
Nūtan sṛṣṭi jāgla bujhi jīban-pare.
Bāje balei bājāo tumi sei garabe,
Ogo prabhu, āmār prāṇe sakal sabe.
Biṣam tomār bahnighāte bāre bāre āmar rāte,
Jvāliye dile nūtan tārā bythāy bhare.

How do you play on the *agniveena*
The sky trembles with the delirium of songs of the stars and light
In the same way in my pains have you touched with your own hands
As if on my life new creations have emerged.
As it plays so do you play on with that pride
O Lord, everything will my heart bear.
With your terrible stroke of fire time and again in night mine
With pains did you enkindle new stars.

41

The light dances in my heart today

Ālo ye āj gān kare mor prāṇe go.
Ke elo mor aṅgane ke jāne go.
Hṛday āmār udās kare keḍe nila ākāś more
Bātās āmāy ānandabāṇ hāne go.
Diganter oi nīl nayaner chāyāte
Kusum yena bikāśe, mor kāyāte.
Mor hṛdayer sugandha ye bāhir hala kāhār khm̐aje
Sakal jīban cāhe kāhār pāne go.

The light dances in my heart today
Who knows who came to my courtyard
Making my heart vacant the sky did snatch me away
The wind throws arrows of joy towards me.
In the shadow of the yonder blue eyes on the horizon
In my body do the flowers as if bloom
The fragrance of my heart appeared in quest of one unknown
O, to whom does the whole life behold.

42

Yonder rings the sound

Tomār duyār kholār dhvani oi go bāje hṛdaymājhe.
Tomār ghare niśi-bhore āgal yadi gela sare
Āmār ghare rāiba tabe kiser lāje
Anek balā balechi, se mithyā balā
Anek calā colechi, se mithyā calā
Āj yena sab pather śeṣe tomār dvāre dm̐āḍāi ese—
Bhuliye yena ney nā more āpan kāje.

Yonder rings the sound of thy opening the door amidst my heart.
If the bar is removed in thy room at night and at dawn
In what shame shall I then remain in my room
Much have I said, lies are they all.
Much have I trekked, false are those trekkings.
At the end of all paths let me stand at thy door today
Let my own work does not make me forgetful.

43

No more late shall I be

Āmār ār habenā deri —
Āmi śunechi oi bāje tomār bherī.
Tumi ki nāth, dn̐āḍīye ācha āmār yābār pathe.
Mane hay ye kṣaṇe kṣaṇe mor bātāyan hate
Tomāy yena heri —
Āmār ār habe nā deri
Āmār kāj hayeche sārā,
Ekhan prāṇe bm̐āśī bājāy sandhyātārā.
Debār mato ya chila mor nāi kichu ār hāte,
Tomār āśīrbāder mālā neba kebal māthe
Āmār lalāṭ gheṛi—
Ār habe nā deri.

No more late shall I be.
Yonder plays on thy bugle that I've heard
Lord, art thou remained standing on my parting way
Methinks at times from my window do I visualize thee
No more late shall I be.
Over is my work
The evening star now plays on the flute in my heart
Nothing else worth giving is with me
Encircling my forehead
On the head shall I adorn thy blissful garland only
No more late shall I be.

44

'Go, shall I go'

Megh baleche 'yaba yaba', rāt baleche 'yāi',
Sāgar bale 'kūl mileche—āmi to ār nāi'.
Duḥkha bale 'rainu cupe tṁāhār pāyer cihnarūpe'.
Āmi bale 'mīlāi āmi ār kichu nā cāi'.
Bhuban bale 'tomār tare āche baraṇmālā',
Gagan bale 'tomār tare lakṣa pradīp jvālā'.
Prem bale ye 'yuge yuge tomār lāgi āchi jege',
Maraṇ bale 'Āmi tomār jīban tarī bāi'

'Go, shall I go', the cloud has said,
the night has declared, 'I'm going',
'The shores are found', says the sea, 'no more am I',
'Let me remain silent', says sorrow, 'like a sign of His feet',
'Let me be in unison', say I, 'no more do I want'.
The world says, 'the garland of reception is for thee',
'For thee', says the sky, 'there are a million lighted lamps',
Love says, 'from years continual do I remain awakened for thee'.
'I ply', says death, 'thy vessel of life'.

45

This boon do I pray

Tomār kāche e bar māgi maraṇ hate yena jāgi gāner sure.
Yemni nayan meli yena mātār stanyasudhā-hena
Nabīn jīban dey go pure gāner sure
Sethāy taru tṛṇa yata
Mātir bṁāśi hate oṭhe gāner mato
Ālok sethā dey go āni
Ākāśer ānandabāṇī,
Hṛday mājhe beḍāy ghure gāner sure.

This boon do I pray to thee, let me rise from death in the tunes of songs
When I open my eyes, like the breast milk of mother
The new life is filled with the tunes of songs
All the trees and grass there
Awake like songs from the flute of the soil
The light there brings along
The message of the joy of the sky
And roams in the heart in the tunes of songs.

46

Stand out

Āpan hate bāhir haye bāire dṁāḍā,
Buker mājhe biśvaloker pābi sāḍā
Ei-ye bipul ḍheu legeche tor mājhete uṭhuk nece,
Sakal parāṇ dik-na nāḍā
Bos-na bhramar, ei nīlimāy āsan laye
Aruṇ-ālor svarṇareṇu-mākhā haye
Yekhānete agādh chuti mel sethā tor ḍānāduti,
Sabār mājhe pābi chāḍā.

Stand out, coming out of yourself
The response of the universe will you have amid your heart.
Let these waves in legion dance within you
Let all lives be moved
Sit down, O bee, with a seat in this sky
Adorned with the golden pollens of sunlight
Spread your two wings where there are unending holidays
Freedom will you enjoy amidst all.

47

This veil would be emaciated

Ei ābaraṇ kṣay habe go kṣay habe,
E dehaman bhūmānandamay habe
Cokhe āmār māyār chāyā ṭuṭbe go,
Biśvakamal prāṇe āmār phuṭbe go,
E jībane tomāri nāth, jay habe.
Rakta āmār biśvatāle nācbe ye,
Hṛday āmār bipul prāṇe bṁācbe ye
Kṁāpbe tomār ālo-bīṇār tāre se,
Dulbe tomār tarāmaṇir hāre se,
Bāsanā tār chaḍiye giye lay habe.

This veil would be emaciated, O emaciated would it be.
Full of the joy of the earth this body and mind would be.
O the shadow of *maya* in my eyes would vanish
The lotus of the world in my heart would bloom
Lord, in this life, thou alone wouldst attain victory
My blood would dance in the rhythm of the world
My heart would live in endless lives
It would tremble in thy string of the *veena* of light,
It would swing in thy necklace of the gems of stars
Its aspirations would end in scatterings.

48

He whom dost thou strike

Puṣpa diye māra yāre cinlonā se maraṇke
Bāṇ kheye ye paḍe se-ye dhare tomār caraṇke
Sabār nīce dhūlār pare phela yāre mṛtyuśare
Se-ye tomār kule paḍe, bhay ki bā tār paḍanke.
Ārāme yār āghāt ḍhākā, kalaṅka yār sugandha
Nayan mele dekhla nā se rudra mukher ānanda
Majla nā se cokher jale, pṁouchala nā caraṇtale
Tile tile pale pale mala ye jan pālaṅke.

He whom dost thou strike with flowers did not know death to meet
The one struck with thy arrows catches hold of thy feet
He whom dost thou pull down on the dust with thy arrow of death.
Falls on thy lap, what fear he bears with this falling breath
He whose wounds are covered with comfort, whose scars are fragrance
Did not see the joy of the furious countenance.
With tears did he not drown himself, nor did he reach at the feet
Who, at every moment and at every step on the adorned bed, did seek the final retreat.

49

All thro' life

Śāra jīban dila ālo sūrya graha cm̐ād
Tomār āśīrbād he prabhu, tomār āśīrbād.
Megher kalas bhare bhare prasādbāri paḍe jhare
Sakal dehe prabhāt bāyu ghucāy abasād—
Tomār āśīrbād he prabhu, tomār āśīrbād.
Tṛṇa ye ei dhūlār pare pāte ām̐calkhāni,
Ei-ye ākāś ciranīrab amṛtamay bāṇī,
Phul ye āse dine dine binā rekhār pathṭi cine,
Ei-ye bhuban dike dike purāy kata sādh—
Tomār āśīrbād he prabhu, tomār āśīrbād.

All thro' life the sun, the planets and the moon
Gave light- thy boon. O Lord, thy boon.
With clouds showering offerings of water from pitchers
The morning air leaves off all tiredness of the body—
Thy boon, O Lord, thy boon.
This grass that spreads its dress-ends on the dust
This sky endlessly silent, a message full of nectar
The flowers that bloom forth every day knowing the path *sans* ever trodden
This world that at every direction fulfils infinite desires—
Thy boon, O Lord, thy boon.

50

O what fear is there

Acenāke bhay kī āmār ore.
Acenākei cine cine uṭhbe jīban bhare
Jāni jāni āmār cenā kono kālei phurābe nā,
Cihnahārā pathe āmāy ṭānbe acin ḍore.
Chila āmār mā acena, nila āmāy kole
Sakal premi acenā go, tāi to hṛday dole
Acenā ei bhuban-mājhe kata surei hrday bāje—
Acenā ei jīban āmār,
Beḍāi tāri ghore.

O what fear is there for me from the unknown
Knowing the unknown over and again, life will be filled in
Know, know I that my knowing no end will know
Towards the path unknown will it pull me on with string unknown
Unknown my mother was, and so she took me on her lap
All love is unknown, and so the heart swings on
Amid this world unknown the heart rings on with tunes unlimited
This life of mine unknown
With delirium do I wander for her.

51

A traveller thou art

Pāntha tumi, pānthajaner sakhā he
Pathe calāi sei to tomāy pāoyā.
Yātrāpather ānandagān ye gāhe
Tāri kanṭhe tomāri gān gāoyā.
Cāy nā se jan pichan-pāne phire,
Bāy nā tarī kebal tīre tīre,
Tuphān tāre dāke akāl nīre
Yār parāne lāgla tomār hāoyā.
Pāntha tumi, pānthajaner sakhā he,
Pathikcitte tomār tarī bāoyā
Duyār khule samuk-pāne ye cāhe
Tār cāoya ye tomār pāne cāoyā
Bipad bādhā kichui ḍare nā se,
Ray nā paḍe kone lābher āśe,
Yābār lāgi man tāri udāse—
Yāoyā se ye tomār pāne yāoyā.

A traveller thou art, O friend of the travelling folk,
To track on the way alone is to meet thee.
With the voice of the singer on the travelling path thy song is sung
Towards the back he looks not
Along the banks alone he plies not the boat
To the shoreless water does the storm beckon him,
Whose life is touched with thy wind.
A traveller thou art, a friend of the travelling folk
Thy plying of the boat is in the mind of the traveller
One who looks ahead opening the door
Looks at thee in reality
Danger or constraint he fears nothing
Nor does he await any bargaining
He waits with a vacant mind for bidding fare-well—
Going in fact is meeting thee.

52

Amid happiness have I seen thee

Sukher mājhe tomāy dekhechi,
Duḥkhe tomāy peyechi prāṇ bhare
Hariye tomāy gopan rekhechi
Peye ābār hārāi milanghore
Cirajīban āmār bīṇā-tāre
Tomār āghāt lāgla bāre bāre
Tāite āmār nānā surer tāne
Prāṇe tomār paraś nilem dhare
Āj to āmi bhay kari ne ār
Līlā yadi phurāy hethākār
Nūtan āloy nūtan andhakāre
Lao yadi bā nūtan sindhupāre
Tabu tumi sei to āmār tumi—
Ābār tomāy cinba nūtan kare

Amid happiness have I seen thee
In sorrow have I found thee with all my heart.
I've kept thee in secrecy by losing.
I lose myself in the delirium of unison again
All thro' life in the string of my *veena*
Thy stroke didst strike again and again
And so in the resonance of my diverse tunes
Thy touch did I hold on in my life
No more do I fear today
If my play here does come to an end
In new light and darkness new
If thou didst receive me on the new sea-coast
Even then thou art that very thee to me—
Again shall I know thee anew.

53

O companion on the way

Pather sāthī, nami bārambār.
Pathik janer laho namaskār.
Ogo bidāy, ogo kṣati, ogo dinaśeṣer pati
Bhāṅa bāsār laho namaskār.
Ogo naba prabhātjyoti, ogo ciradiner gati,
Nūtan āśār laho namaskār.
Jībanrather he sārathi, āmi nitya pather pathī,
Pathe calār laho namaskār.

O companion on the way, I salute thee again and again.
Accept the salutes of the travelling folk.
O Farewell, O loss, O the head of the day's end
Accept the salute of the broken home.
O the new aura of the morning, O the movement of the eternal day,
Accept the salute of new hope.
O the charioteer of the chariot of life, a traveller am I of the path eternal.
Accept the salute to tread on the path.

54

Anew shall I have thee

Tomāy natun korei pāba bale hārāi kṣaṇe kṣaṇ
O mor bhālobāsār dhan
Dekhā debe bale tumi hao ye adarśan
O mor bhālobāsār dhan.
Ogo tumi āmār nao āḍāler, tumi āmār cirakāler—
Kṣaṇakāler līlār srote hao ye nimagan
O mor bhālobāsār dhan.
Āmi tomāy yakhan khm̐uje phiri bhaye km̐āpe man—
Preme āmār ḍheu lāge takhan
Tomār śeṣ nāhi, tāi śūnya seje śeṣ kare dāo āpnāke je—
Oi hāsire dey dhuye mor biroher rodan
O mor bhālobāsār dhan.

Anew shall I have thee, and so do I lose thee time and again
O the wealth of my love.
Thou dost disappear only to appear
O the wealth of my love.
O thou art not behind the curtain,
eternal thou art to me—
Thou dost immerse in the current of transitory play
O the wealth of my love
When I wander seeking thee, my mind does tremble in fear—
Waves adorn my love at that time.
Endless thou art, so empty dost thou end thyself by being vacant.
The waiting of my languishment wash away that smile
O the wealth of my love.

55

In the light of the eye

Cokher āloy dekhechilem cokher bāhire.
Antare āj dekhba yakhan ālok nāhire.
Dharāy yakhan dāo nā dharā hṛday takhan tomāy bharā,
Ekhan tomār āpan āloy tomāy cāhi re.
Tomāy niye khelechilem khelār gharete.
Khelār putul bheṅe geche pralay jhaḍete.
Thāk tabe sei kebal khelā, hok-na ekhan prāṇer melā—
Tārer bīṇā bhāṅla, hṛday-bīṇāy gābi re.

In the light of the eye did I behold beyond the eye
When no light is there, in the heart shall I behold today
When on earth dost thou appear, my heart then is filled in thee
Now in my own light do I desire to have thee.
In the playhouse did I play with thee
In the torrential storm the play-toy is broken apart.
Let that play alone remain aloof, let the feast of life take place now
The *veena* of strings was broken, ah, I sing with the *veena* of the heart.

56

Victory, victory

Habe jay, habe jay habe jay re.
Ohe bīr, he nirbhay.
Jayī prāṇ, ciraprān jayī re ānandagān,
Jayī prem, jayī kṣem, jayī jyotirmay re.
E āṃdhār habe kṣay, have kṣay re,
Ohe bīr, he nirbhay.
Chādo ghum, melo caokh, abasād dūr hok,
Āśār aruṇālok hok abhyuday re.

Victory, victory, O victory shall be.
O brave, O fearless.
Life is victorious, life is eternal, O victorious is the joyous muse
Victory to love, victory to patience, O victorious is the hallowed one.
This darkness would diminish, O diminish would it be
O brave, O fearless,
Leave off slumber, open eyes, let all fatigue be fizzled out
O let the aura of the sun of hope be in efflorescence.

57

My dearest one

Nīśidin mor parāne priyatama mama
Kata nā bedanā diye bāratā pāṭhāle.
Bharile citta mama nitya tumi preme prāṇe gane hāy
Thāki āḍāle.

My dearest one, all day and night in my heart
With what a pain didst thou send thy message,
Ah, thou didst fill my mind in love, life and muse all the time
Remaining behind.

58

The waves of joy

Rahi ṛahi ānandataraṅga jāge.
Rahi rahi prabhu, taba paraśamādhurī
Hṛday mājhe āsi lāge.
Rahi rahi śuni taba caraṇapāta he
Mama pathera āge āge.
Rahi rahi mama manogagana bhātila
Taba prasādarabirāge.

The waves of joy surge at intervals.
At intervals O Lord, the beauty of thy touch
Adorns amidst my heart
At intervals do I listen to thy footsteps
Ahead of my path.
At intervals did the sky of my mind awake
With the aura of thy awarding sun.

59

Bring thy world-embracing seat

Tomār bhubanjoḍā āsankhāni
Hṛday-mājhe bichāo āni.
Rāter tārā, diner rabi āṁdhār-ālor sakal chabi
Tomār ākāś-bharā sakal bāṇī—
Hṛday-mājhe bichāo āni.
Tomār bhubanbīṇār sakal sure
Hṛday parān dāo-nā pure.
Duḥkhasukher sakal haraṣ, phuler paraś, jhaḍer paraś—
Tomār karuṇ śubha udār pāṇi
Hṛday-mājhe dik-nā āni.

Bring thy world embracing seat
And spread on the heart
The stars at night, the sun by day, the pictures all of darkness and light.
All thy message all thro' the sky
Spread on the heart.
With all the tunes of thy *veena* of the world
O fill in the heart and the life
All the laughter of sorrow and happiness, the touch of the flower of the storm—
Let thy hands plaintive, auspicious and generous
Bring forth in the heart.

60

Thine eyes have told me

Tomār nayan āmāy bāre bāre baleche gān gāhibāre
Phule phule tārāy tārāy
Baleche se kon iśārāy
Dibas-rātir mājh-kinārāy dhūsar āloy andhakāre
Gāi ne kena kī kaba tā,
Kena āmār ākulatā—
Byāthār mājhe lukāy kathā, sur ye hārāi akūl pāre.
Yete yete gabhir srote dāk diyecha tarī hate.
Dāk diyecha jhaḍ-tuphāne
Bobā megher bajragāne,
Dāk diyecha maraṇpāne śrabaṇrāter utal dhāre.
Yāi ne kena jāna nā ki—
Tomār pāne mele āṁkhi
Kūler ghāṭe base thāki, path kothā pāi pārābāre.

Thine eyes have told me again and again to sing
With flowers and stars in profusion
With what a beckoning have they said
On the middle edge of day and night, in the darkness of grey light
What shall I say why I sang not
Why my pinings
In pain conceal my words, in the shoreless ends do I lose my tune.
On thy journey thro' deep current thou hast called from the boat
Thou hast called in the storm and speedy wind
In the thunder-song of dumb cloud
Thou hast called towards death in the overflowing drizzling of the *sravan* night
Know ye not why I did not go !
Gazing at thee
Do I remain seated on the bank of the shore,
Where do I get the way in the sea?

61

Wash today

Āj āloker ei jharṇādhārāy dhuiye dāo.
Āpnāke mor lukie-rākhā dulār dhākā dhuiye dāo.
Ye jan āmār mājhe jaḍiye āche ghumer jāle
Āj ei sakāle dhīre dhīre tār kapāle
Ei aruṇ ālor sonār kāṭhi chṁuiye dāo.
Biśvahṛday hate dhāoyā āloy pāgal prabhāt hāoyā,
Sei hāoyāte hṛday āmār nuiye dāo.
Āj nikhiler ānandadhārāy dhuiye dāo,
Maner koṇer malinatā sab dīnatā dhuiye dāo.
Āmar parān-bīṇāy ghumiye āche amṛtagān—
Tār nāiko bāṇī, nāiko chāṇda, nāiko tān
Tāre ānander ei jāgaranī chṁuīye dāo.
Biśvahṛday hate dhāoya prāṇe pāgal gāner hāoyā,
Sei hāoyāte hṛday āmār nuiye dāo.

Wash today with the flow of this fountain of light
Wash this covering of dust to conceal myself.
One entangled within me in the trap of slumber
Be touched by thee on the forehead in the morn
This golden wand of sunlight slowly today.
Rushed from the global heart is the morning air mad in light.
Bend my heart with that air.
Wash today with the flow of the joy of the world,
Wash all dirt on the edge of the mind, all poverty.
In the *veena* of my heart, the nectar-like song is in slumber
No message she has nor has she rhythm or tune.
Let her be touched with this awakener of joy.
Rushed from the global heart is the air of the mad song in the heart
Bend my heart with that air.

62

Ah, O beauty

Ohe sundar, mari mari,
Tomāy kī diye baraṇ kari.
Taba plalgun yena āse
Āji mor paraner pāśe,
Dey sudhārasadhāre-dhāre
Mama añcala bhari bhari.
Madhu samīr digañcale
Āne pulakapūjañjali
Mama hṛdayer pathatale
Yena cañcal āse cali
Mama maner baner śākhe
Yena nikhil kokil dāke
Yena mañjarīdīpaśikhā
Nīl ambare rākhe dhari.

Ah, O Beauty
With what shall I adore thee
As if thy *falgoon* comes
Beside my heart today
With vessels of drinks
My dress-end does it fill and fill.
The sweet air on the edge of horizon
Brings forth offerings of joyous worship—
At the foot of the avenue of my heart
The restless as if does come along.
On the branch of the forest of my mind
The cuckoo of the world as if does coo
As if the flame of the lamp of twigs
Holds on the blue firmament.

63

The day came to an end

Din abasān hala.
Āmār āṁkhi hate astarabir ālor āḍāl tolo.
Andhakārer buker kāche nitya-ālor āsan ache.
Sethāy tomār duyārkhāni kholo.
Sab kathā sab kathār śeṣe ek haye yāk milie ese.
Stabdha bāṇir hṛday-mājhe gabhīr bāṇī āpni bāje,
Sei bāṇīṭi āmār kāne bolo.

The day came to an end.
Raise from my eyes the curtain of the light of the setting sun.
The seat of eternal light is there near the breast of darkness.
Open thy door there.
Let all words in the end of all words be in unison.
Amid the heart of the silent message
The message serene does ring on within.
Tell me that message before my ears.

64

No need of argument

Bujhechi ki bujhi nāi bā se tarke kāj nāi,
Bhālo āmār legeche ye raila sei kathāi.
Bhorer āloy nayan bhare nityake pāi nūtan kare
Kāhār mukhe cāi.
Pratidiner kājer pathe karte ānāgonā
Kāne āmār legeche gān, kareche ānmanā.
Hṛdaye mor kakhan jāni paḍla pāyer cihnakhāni
Ceye dekhi tāi.

No need of argument if I've understood or not
It has appealed me and that alone stands.
In the light of dawn with all eyes do I have the Eternal
At whose countenance do I look.
In the day-to-day journey up and down in the avenue of work
Songs have attuned my ears and made absent-minded.
Know not I when in heart foot-prints did fall
So is it when I behold.

65

O tell me

Āmāy dāo go bale
Se ki tumi āmāy dāo dolā aśāntidole.
Dekhte nā pāi piche theke āghāt diye hṛdaye ke
Ḍheu ye tole.
Mukh dekhi ne tāi lāge bhay- jāni nā ye, e kichu nay.
Muchba āṁkhi, uṭhbo hese-dolā ye dey yakhan ese
Dharbe kole.

O tell me
Is it thee who swingest me in the swing of turmoil
I fail to see one who from behind with a stroke in my heart
Does surge on waves.
I see not the countenance and so do I fear — know not I that it is nothing.
Eyes shall I mop up and in laughter shall I burst out
When one who swings would come and hold me in the lap.

66

Make my heart swing

Āmār Hṛday tomār āpan hāter dole dolāo,
Ke āmāre ki-ye bale bholāo bholāo.
Orā kebal kathār pāke nitya āmāy bm̐edhe rākhe,
Bm̐āśir dāke sakal bm̐ādhan kholāo.
Mane paḍe, kata-nā din rāti
Āmi chilem tomār khelār sāthī.
Ājke tumi temni kare sāmne tomār rākho dhare,
Āmār prāṇe khelār se ḍheu tolāo.

Make my heart swing with the swing of thy own hands
Make me forget whoever tells me anything whatsoever
In the twist of words alone they entangle me for ever
Make all strings open with the call of the flute.
I remember, so many days and nights
Playmate I was of thee.
In the same way do thou hold me today in front of thee
Make that wave of play surge in my heart.

67

In the pretext of play

Khelār chale sājiye āmār gāner bāṇī
Dine dine bhāsāi diner tarīkhāni.
Sroter līlāy bhese bhese sudūre kon acin deśe
Kone ghāṭe ṭhekbe kinā nāhi jāni.
Nāhoy dube gelai, nāhay gelai bā.
Nāhay tule laogo, nāhay pheloibā.
He ajānā, mari mari, uddeśe ei khelā kari,
Ei khelātei āpan mane dhanya māni.

In the pretext of play do I arrange the words of my song
The day's boat do I make afloating by day
Floating in the *lila* of current in an unknown land at a great distance
Know not I if that will harbour at any bank
If it sinks or reaches
If you pick me up or throw away
O unknown, ah, do I play for this purpose
With this play alone do I feel myself blessed within.

68

Thy smile adorns my tune

Āmār sure lāge tomār hāsi,
Yeman ḍheuye ḍheuye rabir kiraṇ dole āsi.
Dibāniśi āmio ye phiri tomār surer khm̐oje,
Haṭhat e man bholāy kakhan tomār bm̐āśi
Āmār sakal kāji raila bāki, sakal śikṣā dilem phm̐āki
Āmār gāne tomāy dharba bale, udās haye yāi ye cale,
Tomār gāne dharā dite bhālobāsi.

Thy smile adorns my tune
Alike sunlight in surging waves
I, too, move in quest of thy tune day and night
All on a sudden does this mind make thy flute forget I know not.
All my work remains undone, all education a void to me
To have a glimpse of thee in my song, I go away in a vacant way
I love to be arrested in thy song.

69

Even now darkness dies not

Ekhano gelonā āṁdhār, ekhano rahila bādhā.
Ekhano maraṇbrata jībane hala nā sādha.
Kabe ye duḥkhajvālā habe re bijaymālā,
Jhalibe arunrāge niśīthrāter kṁādā.
Ekhano nijeri chāyā raciche kata ye māyā.
Ekhano kena-ye miche cāhiche kebali piche,
Cakite bijali-ālo cokhete lāgālo dhṁādā.

Even now darkness dies not, even now does it persist
Even now the askesis of death is not pursued in life
When would the sores of sorrow be the garland of victory
The weepings of midnight would shine in sunlight
Even now the shadow of the very self is creating unending illusion
Even now I know why in vain is my self only looking behind
The sudden lightning shudders the eyes.

70

The *veena* beyond beauty plays on

Arūpbīṇā rūper āḍāle lukiye bāje,
Se bīṇā āji uṭhilo bāji hṛdaymājhe
Bhuban āmār bharila sure, bhed ghuce yāy nikaṭe dūre,
Sei rāgiṇī legeche āmār sakal kāje
Hāte-pāoyār cokhe-cāoyār sakal bṃādhan
Gela keṭe āj, saphal hala sakal kṃādan
Surer rase hāriye yāyāosei to dekhā, sei to pāoyā—
Biraha milan mile gela āj samān sāje.

The *veena* beyond beauty plays on aside in the backdrop of beauty
That *veena* today plays on amid the heart.
With tunes is my world filled, disharmony far or near dispels,
That *ragini* is attuned in all my work
All strings of having in hands and seeing in eyes
Are turn apart, all weepings came to a success
To be lost in the appreciation of tunes—that's seeing, that's having
Languishment and union are in unison today in equal apparel.

71

When thou wouldst dispel

Bāhire bhul hānbe yakhan antare bhul bhaṅbe ki.
Biṣādbiṣe jvale śeṣe tomār prasād maṅbe ki.
Roudradāha hale sārā nāmbe ki or barṣādhārā.
Lājer rāṅā mitle hṛday premer raṅe rāṇbe ki.
Yatai yābe dūrer pāne
Bṁādhan tatai kaṭhin haye ṭānbe nā ki byathār ṭāne.
Abhimāner kālo meghe bādal hāoyā lāgbe bege,
Nayanjaler ābeg takhan konoi bādhā mānbe ki.

When thou wouldst dispel errors outside, would the inherent error be dispelled
Burnt with the poison of sorrow would it beg for thy offerings in the end?
After the burning of the sun, would its flow of rains bring down?
However wouldst thou advance towards the distant
Won't the string pull on hard with the pull of pains?
In the black cloud of langour the rainy wind would speedily blow
Would the flow of tears be tamed by any constraint?

72

Now the sky of the heart

Ebār raṅiye gela hṛdaygagan sṁājher raṅe.
Āmār sakal bāṅī hala magan sṁājher raṅe.
Mane lāge diner pare pathik ebār āsbe ghare,
Āmār pūrṇa habe puṇya lagan sṁājher raṇe.
Astācaler sāgarkūler ei bāṭāse
Kṣaṇe kṣaṇe cakṣe āmār tandrā āse.
Sandhyāyūthīr gandhabhāre pāntha yakhan āsbe dāre
Āmār āpni habe nidrābhagan sṁājher raṅe.

Now the sky of the heart is adorned with the colour of the evening
All my words are immersed in the colour of the evening
The mind feels that at the day's end the traveller would now return home
The auspicious hour of mine would be filled in with the colour of the evening
In this wind of the setting sea-shore
Drowsiness at times looks in my eyes,
When the traveller, burdened with the fragrance of the evening jasmine would arrive at the door
My slumber would be instinctively wiped out with the colour of the evening.

73

In exchange of my langour

Āmār abhimāner badale āj neba tomār mālā.
Āj niśiśeṣe śeṣ kare dii cokher jaler pālā.
Āmār kaṭhin hṛdayṭāre phele dilem pather dhāre,
Tomār caraṇ debe tāre madhur paraś pāṣāṇ-gālā.
Chila āmār āṁdhārkhāni tāre tumii nile ṭāni,
Tomār prem ela ye āgun haye—karla tāre ālā.
Sei-ye Āmār kāche āmi chila sabār ceye dāmi,
Tāre ujāḍ kare sājiye dilem tomār baranḍālā.

In exchange of my langour shall I accept thy garland today.
At the end of night do I finish today the role of tears.
The stern heart of mine do I throw beside the way
Thy feet would favour it with stone-melting pleasing touch
My darkness was there, and it is thee who drawest it near
Thy love came like fire and made it enlightened
The I to me that was the dearest of all,
I poured it all and decorated thy casket of welcome.

74

The vessel of leaves

Pātār bhelā bhāsāi nīre,
Pichon-pāne cāine ne phire
Karma āmạr bojhāi phelā
Khelā āmār calār khelā,
Hayni āmār āsan meḷā
Ghar bṁādhini sroter tīre.
Bṁādhan yakhan bṁādhte āse
Bhāgya amar takhan hāse.
Dhula oḍā hāoyār ḍāke
Path ye ṭene lay āmāke,
Natun natun bṁāke bṁāke,
Gān diye yāi dharitrīre.

The vessel of leaves do I make floating on the water
I look not at the back
My work is to drop the burden
My play is to play how to move
My seat is not yet spread
I built not my home on the water of the current.
When constraints come to clasp
My providence smiles
At the beckoning of dust-blown wind
The way pulls me on
On every new turning
I present the world with songs.

75

Thy chain won't make

Tor śikal āmāy bikal karbe nā.
Tor māre maram marbe na.
Tṁār āpan hāter chāḍciṭhi sei ye
Āmār maner bhitar rayeche ei ye,
Toder dharā āmāy dharbe nā
Ye path diye āmār calācal
Tor praharī tār khṁoj pābe ki bal.
Āmi tṁār duyāre pṁouche gechi re,
More tor duyāre ṭhekābe ki re.
Tor ḍare parān ḍarbe nā.

Thy chain won't make me inactive
Feelings won't die with thy assault.
That passport written in His own hands
Here is it inherent in my mind.
Thy trap won't entrap me.
The avenue while I trek on,
Tell me, would thy watchman trace it out?
At His door have I already arrived.
How would ye stop me at thy door?
My heart won't be afraid of thy intimidation.

76

O fool

Phele rākhlei ki paḍe rabe o abodh.
Ye tār dām jāne se kuḍiye labe o abodh.
O ye kon ratan tā dekh-nā bhābi, or pare ki dhulor dābi.
O hāriye gele tm̐āri galār hār gm̐āthā ye byartha habe.
Or khm̐oj paḍeche jānis ne tā?
Tāi dūt berala hethā sethā.
Yāre karli helā sabāi mili ādar ye tār bāḍiye dili—
Yāre darad dili tār byathā ki sei daradīr prāṇe sabe.

O fool, does anything remain fallen apart if cast aside
O fool, one who knows would pick it up.
Think what a gem it is, what demand does the dust
have upon it.
If he is lost, to prepare the garland for his neck would
be in vain.
Know not that he is being traced out?
So messengers are out everywhere.
Whom all of you neglected is now endeared more
Would the pain for whom you showed your empathy
be endeared in the heart of that Empathiser.

77

Blessed am I

Phul bale, dhanya āmi māṭir pare,
Debatā ogo, tomār sebā āmār ghare.
Janma niyechi dhūlite dayā kare dāo bhulite,
Nāi dhūli mor antare.
Nayan tomār nata karo,
Dalguli kṁāpe tharathara
Caraṇaparaś diyo diyo, dhūlir dhanke karo svargīya—
Dharār praṇām āmi tomār tare.

Blessed am I, says the flower, on earth
O God, thy service is in my room.
On dust am I born, please allow me to forget.
In my heart no dust is there
Bend thine eyes
The petals gently tremble.
Allow, O allow the touch of thy feet, make the treasure
of dust heavenly—
for thee the salutation of the earth am I.

78

Ah, this joyous evening

Āji e ānandasandhyā sundar bikāśe, āhā.
Manda pabane āji bhāse ākāśe
Bidhur byākul madhumādhurī, āhā.
Stabdha gagane grahatārā nīrabe
Kiraṇsaṁgīte sudhā baraṣe, āhā.
Prāṇ man mama dhīre dhīre prasādrase āse bhari,
Deha pulakita udār haraṣe, āhā.

Ah, this joyous evening lovingly manifests.
In the breeze today does effulge in the sky
The agonised restless sweet grandeur, ah.
In the silent sky, silently the planets and the stars
Shower the juice in the songs of light, ah.
My life and the mind are slowly filled in with the juice of offerings.
Joyful is the body with the gracious smile, ah.

79

O my mind

O āmār man, yakhan jāgli nā re
Tor maner mānuṣ elo dvāre.
Tār cale yābār śabda śune bhāṅlo re ghum—
O tor bhāṅlo re ghum andhakāre.
Māṭir pare āṁcal pāti eklā kāṭe niśithrāti.
Tār bṁāśi bāje āṁdhār-mājhe, deki nā ye cakṣe tāre.
Ore, tui jāhāre dili phṁāki khṁuje tāre pāy ki āṁkhi.
Ekhan pathe phire pābi ki re gharer bāhir karli yāre.

O my mind, when you awoke not
The man of your mind came to the door.
With the sound of his parting your slumber was broken
O broken was your slumber in darkness.
Spreading the dress-ends on the earth, the midnight
passes alone
Amid darkness his flute plays on, with eyes do I not
visualize.
O, do the eyes find him out whom you did evade,
Now would you have him back on the way
Whom you drove out of the room ?

80

With my demise

Mor marane habe jay.
Mor jībaṇe tomār paricay.
Mor duḥkha ye rāṅā śatadal
Āj ghirila tomār padatal,
Mor ānanda se ye maṇihār mukuṭe tomār bāṁdhā ray.
Mor tyāge ye tomār habe jay.
Mor preme ye tomār paricay.
Mor dhairya tomār rājpath
Se ye laṅghibe banaparbat,
Mor bīryatomār jayrath tomāri tomāri patākā śire bay.

With my demise would be thy victory
In my life is thy identity
My sorrow, the shining lotus
Does encompass thy foot today
My joy, a necklace of gems, remains entangled in thy headgear.
With my renunciation will be the victory
With my love is thy identity.
My endurance is thy avenue
It would cross o'er forests and mountains
My valour is thy chariot of victory,
Bearing the very flag of thine o'er the head.

81

Now to the distant

Ebār āmāy ḍākle dūre
Sāgar-pārer gopan pure
Bojhā āmār nāmiyechi ye, saṅge āmāy nāo go nije,
Stabdha rāter snigdha sudhā pān karābe tṛṣñāture.
Āmār sandhyāphuler madhu
Ebār ye bhog karbe bṁadhu.
Tārār ālor pradīpkhāni prāṇe āmār jvālbe āni,
Āmār yata kathā chila bhese yābe tomār sure.

Now to the distant did you call on me
In the secret place of sea-shore.
My burden have I brought down, O take me alone with you
To the thirsty would you make drink the pleasant drink of the silent night.
The honey of my evening flower
The bride would enjoy now.
The lamp of starlight would you bring and trim on in my life
All my words that I had would float away with your tunes.

82

Call me or not

Nāi bā ḍāko raiba tomār dvāre,
Mukh phirāle phirba nā eibāre.
Basa tomār pather dhulār pare.
Eḍiye āmāy calbe keman kare–
Tomār tare ye jan gm̐āthe mālā
Gāner kusum jugiye deba tāre
Raiba tomār phasalkheter kāche
Yethāy tomār pāyer cinha āche
Jege raba gabhīr upabāse
Anna tomār āpni yethāy āse—
Yethāy tumi lukiye pradīp jvāla
Base raba sethāy andhakāre.

Call me or not, at thy door shall I remain
If thou turnest back thy face I won't return this time.
On the dust of thy path shall I sit
How would ye avert me—
I would supply one who weaves garlands for thee with flowers of songs
Near the grain-field would I remain,
Where thy footprints adorn.
In poignant fasting would I remain awake
Where thy food automatically comes
Where thou trimmest on the light in secret
In darkness shall I remain seated there.

83

On my journey alone

Yete yete eklā pathe nibeche mor bāti.
Jhaḍ eseche, ore, ebār jhaḍke pelām sāthī.
Akaśkoṇe sarbaneśe kṣṇe kṣṇe uṭhche hese,
Pralay āmār keśe beśe karche mātāmāti.
Ye path diye yetechilem bhuliye dila tāre,
Ābār kothā calte habe gabhīr andhakāre.
Bujhi bā ei bajrarabe nūtan pather bārtā kabe—
Kon purite giye tabe prabhāt habe rāti.

On my journey alone on the way, my light is put off
The storm starts, O, as a comrade did I have the storm.
At times the disaster bursts out laughing in the corner of the sky
On my hair and apparel deluge is dancing intoxicatingly
The way of my journey is made to be forgotten.
Where shall I have to tread on in poignant darkness
May be in this sound of thunder message of a newer avenue would pour forth
In which palace the journey would end and the morning would embrace the night.

84

When the goddess of wealth

Lakṣmī yakhan āsbe takhan kothay tāre dibi re thṁāi.
Dekh re ceye āpan-pāne, padmaṭi nāi, padmaṭi nāi.
Phirche kṁede prabhātbātās, ālok je tār mlān hatāś.
Mukhe ceye ākaś tore śudhāy āji nīrabe tāi.
Kata gopan āśā niye kon se gahan rātriśeṣe
Agādh jaler talā hate amal kṁuḍi uṭhla bhese.
Hala nā tār phuṭe oṭhā, kakhan bheṅe paḍla bṁotā—
Martya-kāche svārgo ya cāy sei mādhuri kothā re pāi.

When the goddess of wealth would come, where would you give her refuge ?
Look at yourself, the lotus is no more, no more is the lotus
The morning wind moves crying, faded and disappointing his light is.
Looking at the face, the sky silently asks you that.
With secret hopes unknown and at the end of dense night unknown
The auspicious bud came out afloating from the infinite depth of water.
It effulged not the peduncle broke unknown—
Where do I have that grace that the heaven demands from the earth ?

85

Trim on yourself

Oi amal hāte rajanī prāte āpni jvālo
Ei to ālo—ei to ālo.
Ei to prabhāt, ei to ākāś, ei to pūjār puṣpabikāś,
Ei to bimal, ei to madhur, ei to bhālo—
Ei to ālo–ei to ālo.
Āṁdhār megher bakṣe jege āpni jvālo
Ei to ālo–ei to ālo.
Ei to jhañjhā taḍit-jvāla, ei to dukher agnimālā,
Ei to mukti, ei to dīpti, ei to bhālo—
Ei to ālo—ei to ālo.

Trim on yourself in that auspicious hand at daybreak
This is light–light this is.
This is morning, the sky this is, this is the effulgence of flowers for worship
This is serene, pleasant this is, this is fine—
This is light–light this is.
Waking upon the breast of dark clouds, trim on yourself
This is light–light this is.
This is hailstorm and the burning of lightning, the firelike garland of sorrow this is,
Freedom this is, this the help, this is fine-
This is light–light this is.

86

In the secret lonely chamber

Mor hṛdayer gopan bijan ghare
Ekela rayecha nīrab śayan-pare—
Priyatama he, jāgo jāgo jāgo.
Ruddha dārer bāhire dm̐āḍāye ami
Ār katakāl emane kātibe svāmī—
Priyatama he, jāgo jāgo jāgo.
Rajanīr tārā uṭheche gagan cheye,
Āche sabe mor bātāyan-pāne ceye—
Priyatama he, jāgo jāgo jāgo.
Jībane āmār saṁgīt dāo āni,
Nīrab rekhonā tomār bīṇār bāṇi—
Priyatama he, jāgo jāgo jāgo.
Milāba nayan taba nayaner sāthe,
Milāba e hāt taba dakṣiṇhāte—
Priyatma he, jāgo jāgo jāgo
Hṛdaypātra sudhāy pūrṇa habe,
Timir km̐āpibe gabhīr ālor rabe—
Priyatama he jāgo jāgo jāgo.

In the secret lonely chamber of my heart
Thou art alone lying on the silent bed–
O dearest, awake awake awake.
Standing outside the closed door am I
How long, O Lord, this would go on
O dearest, awake awake awake.
All thro' the sky the stars at night arise
Everyone is looking towards my window—

O dearest, awake awake awake.
Bring forth music in my life
Make not the message of thy *veena* dumb—
O dearest, awake awake awake.
With thy eyes shall I unite mine
With this hand thy right hand be in unison—
O dearest, awake awake awake.
The cup of the heart will be filled in drink,
Darkness would tremble in the sound of deep light—
O dearest, awake awake awake.

87

All thro' the universe

Biśvajoḍā phm̐ād petecho, kemane dii phm̐āki.
Ādhek dharā paḍechi go, ādhek āche bāki.
Kena jāni āpnā bhule bārek hṛday yāy ye khule,
Bārek tāre ḍhāki
Bahir āmār śukti yena kaṭhin āḅaraṇ—
Antare mor tomār lāgi ekṭi kānnā-dhan.
Hṛday bale tomār dike roibe ceye animikhe,
Cāy nā kena ām̐khi.

All thro' the universe thou hast laden thy trap, how can I be a truant ?
O half I've been trapped, the other half remains
Know not I why the heart forgetful of itself opens,
For once I cover it up,
Like an oyster with a solid shell is my outward frame.
In the mind, a wealth of weeping is there for thee.
To gaze at thee is the saying of the heart
Why not my eyes want ?

88

In this morning

Ājike ei sakālbelāte
Base āchi āmār prāṇer surṭi melāte.
Ākāśe oi aruṇ rāge madhur tān karuṇ lāge,
Bātās māte ālo chāyār māyār khelāte.
Nīlimā ei nilīn hala āmār cetanāy
Sonār ābhā chaḍiye gela maner kāmanāy.
Lokāntarer o pār hate ke udāsī bāyur srote
Bhese beḍāy digante oi megher bhelate.

In this morning today
Seated am I to synchronize my heart's tune.
The pleasing tune in that solar *raga* in the sky appears plaintive
The wind is agog with the illusive game of light and shadow
Immersed is this sky in my consciousness.
The golden aura is spread o'er the desires of the mind.
Who from the yonder shore of the other world wanders afloating in the careless current of the wind
On the vessel of cloud in the distant horizon.

89

In diverse strategies

Tomāri nām balba nānā chale,
Balba ekā bose āpan maner chāyātale.
Balba binā bhāṣāy, balba binā āśāy
Balba mukher hasi diye, balba cokher jale
Binā prayojaner ḍāke ḍākba tomār nām,
Sei ḍāke mor śudhu śudhui purbe manaskām.
Śiśu yeman māke nāmer neśāy ḍāke,
Balte pāre ei sukhetei māyer nām se bale.

In diverse strategies shall I tell thy name.
Sitting alone under the shade of my own mind shall I tell.
Sans language shall I tell, I shall tell bereft of hope
With the laughter of the face shall I tell
I shall tell with tears
At the call *sans* need shall I call on thy name.
With that call my desires would by itself be fulfilled
As a child calls on its mother in the craze of calling,
With this very happiness can it tell,
Tells the name of its mother.

90

Infinite wealth thou hast

Asīm dhaṇ to āche tomār, tāhe sādh nā meṭe.
Nite cāo tā āmār hāte kaṇāy kaṇāy bṁeṭe.
Diye tomār ratanmaṇi āmāy karle dhani—
Ekhan dvāre ese dāko, rayechi dvār eṁṭe.
Āmāy tumi karbe dātā, āpni bhikṣu habe—
Bisvabhuban mātla ye tāi hasir kalarabe
Tumi raibe nā oi rathe nāmbe dhulāpathe
Yug-yugānta āmār sāthe calbe hṁeṭe hṁeṭe.

Infinite wealth thou hast, yet thy desires remain unfulfilled
Thou dost want to have that from a division of every bit in thy hands.
Thou hast made one rich by offering thy jewels and gems—
Call on me at my door now, I am in closed door.
Thou wouldst make me a donor, a mendicant wouldst thou be.
So the whole universe is agog with the sound of laughter.
On that chariot thou wouldst not remain.
On the dusty way wouldst thou come down
And go on walking along with me from age beyond age.

91

The hurricane of laughter

Prāṅe khuśir tuphān uṭheche
Bhay-bhābanār bādhā ṭuṭeche
Duḥkhake āj kaṭhin bale jaḍiye dharte buker tale
Udhāo haye hṛday chuṭeche
Hethāy kāro ṭhṁāi habe nā mane chila ei bhābanā,
Duyār bheṅe sabāi juṭeche.
Yatan kare āpnāke ye rekhechilem dhuye meje,
Ānande se dhulāy luṭeche.

The hurricane of laughter has surged in life
Gone are the constraints of fear and thought
To clasp sorrow under the breast as a stern one
The heart has run away in disappearance.
No shelter would be here for any one.
So was the thought in mind
Breaking the door open, everyone has assembled.
So caressingly as I kept myself wasted and brushed,
Now he is in the dust in joy.

92

When like a flower

Jāban yakhan chila phuler mato
Pāpḍi tāhār chila śata śata
Basante se hata yakhan dātā
Jhariye dita du-cārṭe tār pātā
Tabuo ye tār bāki raita kata
Āj bujhi tār phal dhareche, tāi
Hāte tāhār adhik kichu nāi.
Hemante tār samay hala ebe
Pūrṇa kare āpnāke se debe,
Raser bhāre tāi se abanata.

When like a flower was life
Hundreds of petals it had.
When in spring a donor it became
Two or four leaves did it drop down
Even then so many did it have.
May be it is enriched with fruit, and so
Nothing more does it have within itself.
Now in the late autumn it is time
To deliver itself in fulness.
So it is bent down with the burden of juice.

93

Not a pleasant game

Nay e madhur khela—
Tomāy āmāy sārājīban sakāl-sandhyābela nay e madhur khelā.
Katabār ye nibhla bāti, garje ela jhaḍer rāti—
Saṃsārer ei dolāy dile saṃśayeri ṭhelā.
Bāre bāre bṁādh bhaṅiya banyā chuṭeche.
Dāruṇ dine dike dike kānnā uṭheche.
Ogo rudra, duḥkhe sukhe ei kathāṭi bājlo buke—
Tomār preme āghāt āche, nāiko abahelā.

Not a pleasant game it is—
Between you and me all thro' life from morn till evening not a pleasant game it is.
So many times was the lamp put out, roaring came the stormy night
In this swing of the world did you deliver a push of doubt.
Time and again flood has swept over embankments
Wailings have surged on all around in days of agonies
O furious, this tuned on in the heart in sorrow and happiness.
There is a hit but no neglect in your love.

94

In thy assembly

Sabhāy tomār thāki sabār śāsane,
Āmār kaṇṭhe sethāy sur kṁepe yāy trāsane.
Tākāy sakal loke
Takhan dekhte nā pāi cokhe
Kothāy abhay hāsi hāsa āpan āsane.
Kabe āmār e lajjābhay khasābe,
Tomār eklā gharer nirālāte basābe.
Yā śonābār āche
Gāba oi caraṇer kāche
Dvārer āḍāl hate śone bā keu nā śone.

In thy assembly do I remain under everyone's rule
Tune in my voice trembles there in fear.
Everyone looks
Then in my eyes I cannot see
Where dost thou laugh with a fearless smile on thy seat
When wouldst thou wipe out this bashfulness and fear
within me.
In the solitude of thy single room make me seated
Whatever to make thee listen
At the end of thy feet shall I sing
Someone listens or not from the curtain of the door.

95

When my pain

Āmār byajthā yakhan āne āmāy tomār dvāre
Takhan āpni ese dvār khule dāo, ḍāko tāre
Bāhupāśer kāṇāl se ye, caleche tāi sakal tyeje
Kṁātār pathe dhāy se tomār abhisāre.
Āmār byathā yakhan bājāy āmāy bāji sure—
Sei gāner ṭāne pāro nā ār raite dūre.
Luṭiye paḍe se gān mama jhaḍer rāter pākhi-sama,
Bāhir haye esa tumi andhakāre.

When my pain brings me at thy door
Thou dost open the door thyself and call him.
A beggar of the arms' embrace as he is, and so he is trekking on leaving all
He rushes towards the thorny way for thy renunciation.
When my pain plays me on in tune then do I play on—
No more dost thou remain away with the pull of that song
Like a bird in a stormy night that song of mine sweeps down.
In darkness come ye out.

96

Lord as soon as thy *veena*

Prabhu, *tomār bīṇā yemni bāje*
āṁdhār- mājhe
amni phoṭe tārā.
Yena *sei bīṇāṭi gabhīr tāne*
āmār prāṇe
bāje temnidhārā.
Takhan *nūtan sṛṣṭi prakāś habe*
kī gourabe
hṛday-andhakāre
Takhan *stare stare ālokrāśi*
uṭhbe bdāsi
cittagaganpāre.
Yakhan *tomāri soundaryachabi*
ogo kabi
āmāy paḍbe āṁkā—
Takhan *bismayer rabenā śīmā*
ei mahimā
ār yābenā ḍhākā.
Takhan *tomāri prasanna hāsi*
paḍbe āsi
nabajīban-pare.
Takhan *ānanda-amṛte taba*
dhanya haba
ciradiner tare.

Lord, as soon as thy *veena* plays on amid darkness, stars bloom.
As if in poignant strain does that *veena*
in my mind play on in the same fashion.
Then with what a glory new creation would manifest in the darkness of the heart.
Then streams of light by steps would appear
on the shore of the sky of the mind.
Then thy very picture of beauty O poet, would be drawn on me.
Then endless would be wonder, that glory no more would be covered.
Then thy very gracious smile would fall on the life anew.
Then with thy nectar of joy would I be thankful for ever.

97

The night when my doors

Ye rāte mor duyārguli bāṅla jhaḍe
Jāni nāi to tumi ele āmār ghare
Sab ye haye gela kālo, hibe gela dīper ālo,
Ākāś-pāne hāt bādālem kāhār tare.
Andhakāre rainu paḍe svapan māni.
Jhad je tomār jayadhvajā tāi ki jāni!
Sakālbelāy ceye dekhi, dṃāḍiye ācha tumi e ki,
Ghar-bharā mor śūnyatāri buker pare.

The night when my doors were broken by the storm
Thou didst come to my room I know not.
Everything turned black, the light of the lamp was extinguished
For whom did I extend my hands towards the sky.
In darkness did I remain laiden accepting dreams
The storm is thy flag of victory, ah, do I know that !
Looking in the morn I see ah, thou art there standing
On the breast of the void all around my room.

98

The wind touches

Hāoyā lāge gāner pāle—
Mājhi āmār, boso hāle
Ebār chāḍā pele bṁāce
Jibantarī ḍheuye nāce
Ei bātāser tāle tāle
Din giyeche, ela rāti,
Nāi keha mor ghāṭer sāthī
Kāṭo bṁādhan, dāo go chādi —
Tārār āloy deba pāḍi
Sur jegeche yābār kāle.

The wind touches in the sail of songs—
O my oarsman, be seated on the oars-stand.
Now with the freedom of departure
The life's boat dances in waves
With the rhythm of this wind
Gone is the day, the night comes
None is there as a companion on the
bank for me
Cut off the string, O please start
In the light of stars shall I cross o'er,
Tunings adorn at the time of parting.

99

In the morning

Sakāl-sṁāje
Dhāy ye orā nānā kāje.
Āmi kebal base āchi āpan mane kṃāṭā bāchi
Pather mājhe sakāl-sṁāje.
E path beye
Se āse, tāi āchi ceye
Katai kṃāṭā bāje pāye, katai dhulā lāge gāye—
Mori lāje, sakāl-sṁāje.

In the morning and in the evening
In diverse work do they rush on.
Only I remain seated, screening thorns in my own mind
Amidst the way in the morning and in the evening
Trekking on this way
He comes, so I remain a-looking
So many thorns stick to the feet, so much dust sprinkles
on the body
In shame do I die in the morning and in the evening.

100

As my life is going on

Jiban āmār calche yeman temni bhābe
Sahaj kaṭhin dvandve chande cale yābe.
Calār pathe dine rāte dekhā habe sabār sāthe—
Tāder āmi Cāba, tārā āmāy cābe.
Jiban āmār pale pale emni bhābe
Duḥkhasukher raṅe raṅe raṅiye yābe.
Raṅer khelār sei sabhāte khele ye jan sabār sāthe
Tāre āmi cābo, seo āmāy cābe.

As my life is going on
So would it go on in conflicts easy and tough and in rhythm.
On my journey day and night I would encounter all—
I would have them, they, too, would have me.
At every moment my life would in this way
Go on decorating with the colours of sorrow and happiness,
One who plays with all in that assembly of the gem of colours
Him would I have, He, too, would have me.